Table of Contents

Table of Contents

About the Author

Having been a West Ham fan for over 40 years I have always been interested in the History of this great club. Despite never seeing the club win a trophy myself it is so special to me in a way that cannot possibly be defined. It's like someone you love that doesn't quite seem to love you in the same way, but you cannot stop trying.... Because one day they may well fulfill your every need.

Steeped in history the club has been part of my family since its formation and as a 4th generation Hammer, I am now attending games with my children – the 5th generation. For all West Hams on field failings, it really doesn't matter to me. I moan with the best of them, I moan with the rest of them, but they will be part of my DNA until the day I pass this world – and when I leave, I will be safe in the knowledge that the generations of fans will continue forevermore

I have put this quizbook together as a bit of fun and a true knowledge test – but also as an educational tool in a manner that doesn't involve lots of reading. The main events of the history of my club are all included, and I hope you can enjoy – but also learn as you go.

Long Live the Boleyn – West Ham 'til I die

THIS IS THE WEST HAM QUIZBOOK

The Quizbook is intended to take you through the History of West Ham United Football Club. (Everything is correct at date of writing 2023)

It starts with the early years and will follow a rough chronology through to the present day. The early questions are naturally harder – but oh so important to understand the importance of the history of West Ham.

The book includes sections of multiple-choice questions in blocks of 10. In between the multiple-choice questions there are a variety of other questions I have put together in slightly different formats.

You will be asked to name the player, remember nicknames, remember as many players as possible in some of West Hams biggest matches. Some of them will take time and need to be thought about. If you take time to test your memory you will be rewarded

Each section can be cross referenced against the answers provided towards the end of the book.

Grab a drink, something to eat and a pencil and enjoy the quizbook – or take it to your friends and fill out together – or quiz your best mate who claims to know everything about West Ham and see how much they truly know.

Most of all – enjoy and remember the history and traditions of our great club.

B Demure

The West Ham Quizbook

The Early History of West Ham United

1. Before West Ham were formed, they were known as Thames Ironworks. What year did Thames Ironworks form?
   a. 1901 ☑
   b. 1877 ☐
   c. 1895 ☐
   d. 1888 ☐

2. Prior to moving to the Boleyn Ground where did West Ham play their football matches?
   a. The Recreation Ground ☐
   b. The Memorial Grounds ☐
   c. Newham Fields ☐
   d. Plaistow Park ☐

3. What year did West Ham move to the Boleyn?
    a. 1901 ☐
    b. 1904 ☐
    c. 1899 ☐
    d. 1895 ☐

4. What was the Boleyn Ground originally named when West Ham first moved there?
    a. The Bow Bell Green ☐
    b. The Iron Gate ☐
    c. The Castle ☐
    d. Green Street Ground ☐

5. Who did West Ham play in the first game at their new home?
    a. Wellingborough ☐
    b. Luton Town ☐
    c. Millwall ☐
    d. New Brompton ☐

6. Who was appointed manager of West Ham in 1902 starting a 30-year spell as manager?
    a. Barry Coates ☐
    b. Steve Chalmers ☐
    c. Syd King ☐
    d. Malcolm Archer ☐

7. Which league did West Ham play in between 1899 and 1915?
    a. London East League ☐
    b. Southern Football League ☐
    c. Isthmian National League ☐
    d. Premier Central League ☐

8. Following the end of World War I West Ham were elected into the Football league's second division. What year did they gain promotion to the top division?
    a. 1919 ☐
    b. 1920 ☐
    c. 1923 ☐
    d. 1928 ☐

9. In 1920 West Ham signed a Centre forward for a sum of £50 from Wellingborough Town - He went on to score 326 goals for the club. What was his name?
    a. Syd Puddefoot ☐
    b. Vic Watson ☐
    c. Billy Moore ☐
    d. Dick Leafe ☐

10. Also, in 1920 a 20-year-old Outside Left born in Doncaster joined the club. He went on to score 159 goals playing 505 times. What was his name?

    a. Jimmy Ruffell ☐

    b. David Lloyd ☐

    c. Bill Joyce ☐

    d. Stan Foxall ☐

(ANSWERS CAN BE FOUND ON PAGE 77)

SECTION TWO

NAME THE FAMOUS HAMMERS

1. Signed for a fee of £300,000 from Birmingham City in 1988 this player made over 260 appearances for the club in two spells between 1988 and 1999 separated by a season on Merseyside with Liverpool.

2 This player scored 78 goals for West Ham between 1977 and 1982. Born in Heywood Greater Manchester his no nonsense style earnt him the nickname "Psycho".

3   This Goalkeeper came from somewhere near Moscow. In fact, he was born in Czechoslovakia in 1961 he went on to make 40 international appearances for his country and played 318 times for West Ham before leaving in 1998 and ended his career at QPR in 2001.

┌─────────────────────────────────────┐
│   │
│   │
└─────────────────────────────────────┘

4   A vital part of the 2011/12 promotion campaign. This player signed from Newcastle scoring 12 goals that season taking the number 4 shirt and becoming club captain. He spent 5 seasons at West Ham playing over 150 games.

┌─────────────────────────────────────┐
│   │
│   │
└─────────────────────────────────────┘

5 Signed for a club record of £10.75 million from Wolverhampton Wanderers in 2011 this left winger made 78 appearances for the club. He joined Norwich initially on loan in 2014 before signing permanently for a reported fee of £2.6 million in 2015.

6 A Centre back that came through the youth ranks making his Debut at the age of 17 on May 5th 1996 coming onto the field to replace Tony Cottee. He went on to make 127 appearances for the club before a big money transfer to Leeds United in 2000

7 A true legend who made 663 appearances for the club lifting the FA cup twice and returning for a spell as manager in 1990 before a brief spell as manager of Millwall in 1997-98.

8   Hammer of the year three times in a row (08-09, 09-10, 10-11) this player signed from Newcastle for £7 million before leaving to join Tottenham Hotspur for £5.5 million in 2011.

9   Signed for West Ham in 2015 this player filled numerous positions but settled as a striker and became the clubs highest Premier League Goalscorer when he scored a brace against Leicester City in 2021.

10 A combative no-nonsense midfielder who was booked 66 times (along with 3 red cards) in his Hammers career. He spent 9 years at West Ham between 1994 and 2003 playing 176 after signing from Swindon Town

(ANSWERS CAN BE FOUND ON PAGE 78)

WEST HAM UNITED
1980 FA CUP XI

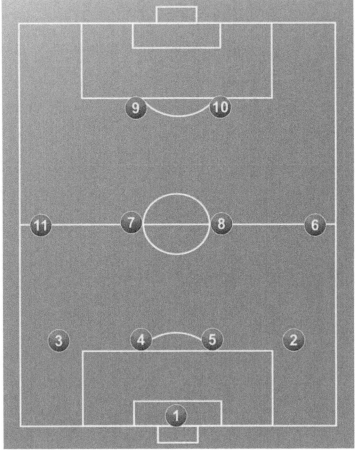

(The numbers used are to represent positions only – they are not accurate as worn on the day)

How many of the West Ham 1980 FA CUP XI final winners can you name? Initials used to give you a helping hand:

1. PP	
2. RS	
3. FL	
4. BB	
5. AM	
6. AD	
7. PA	
8. SP	
9. DC	
10. TB	
11. GP	

Bonus point available. Can you name the substitute used?

12. PB	

(ANSWERS CAN BE FOUND ON PAGE 79)

SECTION FOUR

WEST HAM UNITED 1920s-1950s

1. In what year did West Ham contest their first ever FA Cup Final?
   - a. 1921 ☐
   - b. 1936 ☐
   - c. 1925 ☐
   - d. 1923 ☐
2. Who were West Hams opponent in this cup final and what was the final score?
   - a. Liverpool 2-0 West Ham United ☐
   - b. West Ham United 2-0 Sheffield U ☐
   - c. Bolton Wanderers 2-0 West Ham ☐
   - d. West Ham 3-1 Tottenham Hotspur ☐

3. This FA Cup final was the first to be held at Wembley Stadium and suffered from mass overcrowding and as such is often referred to as what?

    a. The Big Match ☐

    b. Battle of Wembley ☐

    c. The White Horse Final ☐

    d. Wembley Riot Final ☐

4. In the 1924/25 season West Ham won the London Challenge cup 2-1. Who were their opponents that day?

    a. Crystal Palace ☐

    b. Clapton Orient ☐

    c. Charlton Athletic ☐

    d. Leyton ☐

5. West Ham were relegated from the top division in 1931/32 finishing bottom (22nd) after being relegated how did they fare in the second division in 1932/33?

    a. 1st ☐

    b. 4th ☐

    c. 13th ☐

    d. 20th ☐

6. Due to the outbreak of World War II the football league and FA cup were suspended. A regional competition begun 6 weeks later West Ham won the competition on 8th June 1940 at Wembley. Defeating Blackburn Rovers 4-3. What was this competition called?

   a. The Great War Cup ☐
   b. Churchill Trophy ☐
   c. 1940 trophy ☐
   d. Football League War Cup ☐

7. What happened to the Boleyn Ground during World War II?

   a. Part of the stadium was demolished for metal ☐
   b. It was used as a training camp for soldiers ☐
   c. It was partially destroyed by a German bomb ☐
   d. Used to house residents made homeless by bombing ☐

8. In 1950 which manager took control of the club? He set about scouting and developing the best local talent – starting what would become known as 'The Academy of Football'
    a. Mark Phillips ☐
    b. Steve Ward ☐
    c. Ted Fenton ☐
    d. John Cross ☐

9. Defender Malcolm Allison was a vital part of 1950s West Ham – he famously used Cassettaris Café on the Barking Road for what reason?
    a. Creating the perfect diet for players ☐
    b. Would cook all the players lunch after training ☐
    c. Ran a gambling club to boost morale ☐
    d. Discussing Match tactics and formations ☐

10. Allison was diagnosed with tuberculosis in 1957 and had to have a lung removed. Due to his absence a young 17-year-old made his debut for West Ham in September 1958 – what was his name?

    a. Ray Stewart ☐

    b. Bobby Moore ☐

    c. John Lyall ☐

    d. Geoff Hurst ☐

(ANSWERS CAN BE FOUND ON PAGE 80)

FIVE CLUES TO NAME A HAMMERS PLAYER.

MORE POINTS ARE AWARDED DEPENDING ON WHEN YOU GET THE CORRECT ANSWER. ONLY LOOK AT ONE CLUE AT A TIME AND WRITE YOUR GUESS IN THE ANSWER COLUMN ACCORDINGLY. 5 POINTS AWARDED IF YOU GET IT CORRECT AFTER CLUE 1 ALL THE WAY DOWN TO 1 POINT IF YOU GUESS THE ANSWER CORRECTLY AFTER QUESTION FIVE

CLUE ONE	ANSWER (5 POINTS)
1. Signed for £300,000 in 1995	
2. Signed from Barnsley in 2012	
3. Signed in 2015 for £10.7m	
4. Signed for £300,000 in 1998	
5. Youth Product who debuted in '99	

CLUE TWO	ANSWER (4 POINTS)
1. Left Winger made 69 appearances	
2. Scored 19 goals in 61 appearances	
3. Scored 15 goals in 60 appearances	
4. Scored 3 goals in 56 appearances	
5. Scored 18 goals in 187 appearances	

CLUE THREE	ANSWER (3 POINTS)
1. Left to Join Birmingham City in 2000 for a fee of £1.7 million	
2. Scored 12 goals in the 11/12 season despite only joining in January	
3. Left for £25 million in 2017	
4. Left on a free transfer in 2000	
5. Sold for £6.6 million after West Ham were relegated in 2003	

CLUE FOUR	ANSWER (2 POINTS)
1. Scored a stunning 30 yarder against Newcastle at St James Park	
2. A Portuguese national but never played for the national team	
3. 2015/16 Hammer of the year	
4. Had played 152 times for Liverpool before joining West Ham	
5. Went on to join Chelsea as well as Liverpool	

CLUE FIVE	ANSWER (1 POINT)
1. Made 60 appearances for Australia	
2. Scored the Play off final winner (11/12)	
3. French International playing 38 times	
4. Tough left back	
5. Returned to West Ham in 2012	

(ANSWERS CAN BE FOUND ON PAGE 81)

SECTION SIX

WEST HAM UNITED 1960s

1. In 1961 who did West Ham appoint as manager who remained at the club until 1974?
    a. Ron Greenwood ☐
    b. Ted Fenton ☐
    c. Geoff Pike ☐
    d. John Lyall ☐
2. In 1964 West Ham won the FA cup 3-2 against which club?
    a. Manchester United ☐
    b. Arsenal ☐
    c. Preston North End ☐
    d. Bolton Wanderers ☐
3. The 1964 FA cup win came courtesy of a late winner scored by which player?
    a. Bobby Moore ☐
    b. John Bond ☐
    c. Geoff Hurst ☐
    d. Ronnie Boyce ☐

4. After winning the FA cup West Ham qualified for the European Cup Winners Cup competition. How far did they get?

    a. Quarter Final ☐

    b. Winners ☐

    c. Semi Final ☐

    d. Finalists ☐

5. What award did West Ham United win in 1965?

    a. Sports Personality team of the year award ☐

    b. FIFA team of the year ☐

    c. FIFA fair play award ☐

    d. UEFA team of the year award ☐

6. In 1966 England won the World Cup Final. West Hams Geoff Hurst scoring a famous hattrick. Hurst got his place in the team after which player suffered an injury against France?

    a. George Cohen ☐

    b. Roger Hunt ☐

    c. Bobby Charlton ☐

    d. Jimmy Greaves ☐

7. After returning as a national hero from the World Cup in 1966 how many goals did Geoff Hurst score in the 1966/67 season?

    a. 41 ☐

    b. 17 ☐

    c. 7 ☐

    d. 28 ☐

8. In 1969 the East Stand was redeveloped, and the old wooden stand was demolished. What was this affectionately known as?

    a. The Old Girl ☐

    b. The Chicken Run ☐

    c. The tree house ☐

    d. The Boleyn Boys stand ☐

9. World Cup Winner Martin Peters was a vital part of West Hams success in the 1960s. Playing 364 games between 1961 and 1970. How many goals did he score during this period?

    a. 175 ☐

    b. 78 ☐

    c. 140 ☐

    d. 100 ☐

10. Martin Peters left West Ham to join which club to become Britain's first £200,000 footballer?

    a. Tottenham Hotspur ☐

    b. Liverpool ☐

    c. Manchester United ☐

    d. Arsenal ☐

(ANSWERS CAN BE FOUND ON PAGE 82)

WEST HAM PLAYER NICKNAMES

1. Who was known as 'The Terminator'?
   a. Ron Greenwood ☐
   b. Ludek Miklosko ☐
   c. Alvin Martin ☐
   d. Julian Dicks ☐

2. Who had the nickname 'Pop' due to his lack of hair at a young age?
   a. John Moncur ☐
   b. Bryan Robson ☐
   c. Martin Peters ☐
   d. John Sissons ☐

3. Who was nicknamed 'Razor' after an American Boxer who shared the same surname?
   a. Keith Rowland ☐
   b. Winston Reid ☐
   c. Neil Ruddock ☐
   d. Mark Robson ☐

4. Who was nicknamed 'The Ginger Pele'?
    a. James Collins ☐
    b. Steve Lomas ☐
    c. John Hartson ☐
    d. David Martin ☐
5. Who was nicknamed 'Tonka'– he is still considered by many to be the clubs greatest ever penalty taker?
    a. Mark Noble ☐
    b. Paul Kitson ☐
    c. James Tomkins ☐
    d. Ray Stewart ☐
6. Nicknamed 'The Hammer' because of his fierce shot this player joined the club in 2010 and with his nickname could have been the perfect match. But his best years were behind him and due to injuries only made 13 appearances for the club
    a. Don Hutchison ☐
    b. Thomas Hitzlsperger ☐
    c. Ray Houghton ☐
    d. Marlon Harewood ☐

7. Nicknamed 'The General' this player joined in 2018 and played 62 times before heading to Russia and Dynamo Moscow in 2021
    a. Carlos Sanchez ☐
    b. Felipe Anderson ☐
    c. Victor Moses ☐
    d. Fabian Balbuena ☐
8. Known as 'The Little Pea' scored 17 goals in 63 appearances for the club
    a. Javier Hernandez ☐
    b. Sebastian Haller ☐
    c. Javier Mascherano ☐
    d. Savio Nsereko ☐
9. This player was nicknamed 'The Rhino' due to the way he charged out of defence with the ball
    a. Rio Ferdinand ☐
    b. Bobby Moore ☐
    c. Marc Rieper ☐
    d. David Unsworth ☐

10. Although he never played a senior game for West Ham this academy product had to be included in this for probably the best nickname in football history. Who was known as 'one size'?

    a. Fitz Hall ☐

    b. John Sissons ☐

    c. Lionel Scaloni ☐

    d. Alex Song ☐

(ANSWERS CAN BE FOUND ON PAGE 83)

WEST HAM UNITED 1970s

1. Geoff Hurst was top goalscorer in the 1970/71 season. Clyde Best scored 23 goals in the 1971/72 season. But who was top scorer in 72/73 with 28 goals after his arrival from Newcastle?

    a. Bryan Robson ☐

    b. Billy Bonds ☐

    c. Bill Jennings ☐

    d. David Cross ☐

2. Who became West Ham manager in 1974?

    a. Ron Atkinson ☐

    b. John Lyall ☐

    c. Billy Jennings ☐

    d. Graham Taylor ☐

3. Bobby Moore left West Ham United in 1974. Which London Club did he sign for?

    a. Tottenham Hotspur ☐

    b. Chelsea ☐

    c. Fulham ☐

    d. Queens Park Rangers ☐

4. Who became West Hams official club captain following the departure of Bobby Moore?

    a. Vic Watson ☐

    b. Bryan Robson ☐

    c. Billy Bonds ☐

    d. Alvin Martin ☐

5. The FA Cup final of 1975 against Fulham was won by two goals from which young player?

    a. Frank Lampard Sr ☐

    b. Tommy Taylor ☐

    c. Pay Holland ☐

    d. Alan Taylor ☐

6. 1975/76 saw West Ham in the European Cup Winners Cup. Ultimately ending in disappointment in the final against which club?

    a. Celtic ☐

    b. Eintracht Frankfurt ☐

    c. Anderlecht ☐

    d. Fiorentina ☐

7. Which player Impressed for the opposition in the Cup Winners Cup Final so much that West Ham brought him to East London a few years later?

    a. Rob Hesenbrink ☐

    b. Steffan Muller ☐

    c. Hugo Broos ☐

    d. Francois Van der Elst ☐

8. In 1976 West Ham signed a 20-year-old from Southall who went on to play well over 400 times for the club and go down as one of the biggest legends to don the Claret and Blue.

    a. Alan Devonshire ☐

    b. Paul Parker ☐

    c. Geoff Pike ☐

    d. Billy Jennings ☐

9. What happened at the end of the 1977/78 season?

    a. West Ham Qualified for the UEFA cup ☐

    b. West Ham finished in their highest ever position ☐

    c. West Ham were relegated ☐

    d. West Ham won the FA cup ☐

10. Who did West Ham sign for a then World Record transfer for a goalkeeper of £565,000 in 1979?

    a. Les Sealey ☐

    b. Mervyn Day ☐

    c. Ernie Gregory ☐

    d. Phil Parkes ☐

(ANSWERS CAN BE FOUND ON PAGE 84)

SECTION NINE

WEST HAM UNITED ENGLAND INTERNATIONALS

Since 1970 nine players have played 10 or more games for England whilst they were a West Ham player – clues below to help you name them all:

1. This man played 47 times for England between 1974 and 1982 scoring 5 goals. He spent 18 years at West Ham between 1966 and 1984 scoring the winner in a cup final.

2. No nonsense scouse Centre back played 598 games for West Ham between 1978 and 1996 and gained 17 England caps during his career.

3. From no nonsense to a majestic Centre back who played 10 times for England whilst at West Ham but went on to gain 81 caps, the majority whilst playing for Manchester United.

```



```

4. A true generational talent who played 56 times for England but only 10 of those whilst at West Ham. His last England Cap came in 2010 when he left West London to move to the Northwest of England

```



```

5. This stopper signed from Aston Villa in 2001. His England career spanned 13 years where he amassed 64 England caps. 17 of those during a three-year spell at West Ham

```



```

6. A winger who scored some brilliant goals in his career. He represented England 11 times whilst a West Ham Player. He left to join Manchester City in 2003 but arguably the best football of his career was played at Queens Park Rangers

> [   ]

7. A Centre back who played 131 times for West Ham over four years and played 14 times for England during this period. He was named as West Ham captain in 2009 before departing for Stoke City in 2011

> [   ]

8. Another keeper who was knocking on the England door for years. He managed to accrue 12 England caps. He famously had "England's number 6" embroidered onto his goalkeeping gloves in ode to a sarcastic chant from the West Ham faithful

> [   ]

9. 39 England caps at just 23 years old this youth product who joined from Chelsea at 15 played a pivotal role in England's run to the European Champions finals ultimately ending in defeat against Italy.

```
┌─────────────────────────────────────────┐
│                                         │
│                                         │
└─────────────────────────────────────────┘
```

10. This last player only managed eight England appearances. But deserves an honorable mention as he should have had many more. He got his eight caps between 1980 and 1983. In early 1984 he snapped three ligaments in his knee

```
┌─────────────────────────────────────────┐
│                                         │
│                                         │
└─────────────────────────────────────────┘
```

(ANSWERS CAN BE FOUND ON PAGE 85)

SECTION TEN

WEST HAM UNITED 1980s

1. In 1980 West Ham won the FA cup 1-0 against Arsenal thanks to a Trevor Brooking header. What was significant about this victory?

    a. Arsenals first ever defeat in a final ☐

    b. Trevor Brookings 100th career goal ☐

    c. First time a club outside the top tier won the FA cup ☐

    d. West Ham had never beaten Arsenal before ☐

2. In 1983 West Ham recorded their highest ever win in the Football League Cup v Bury – what was the score?

    a. 8-1 ☐

    b. 8-0 ☐

    c. 9-1 ☐

    d. 10-0 ☐

3. Who was made West Ham Captain in 1984 when Billy Bonds first retired? (Bonds returned to the squad when several injuries left them struggling)
   a. David Cross ☐
   b. Paul Goddard ☐
   c. Tony Cottee ☐
   d. Alvin Martin ☐

4. Which player made their debut in 1984 after signing from Fulham for £200,000. He went on to make 300 league appearances for the club before joining Blackburn in 1994 making 15 appearances for the 94/95 title winners
   a. Colin Hendry ☐
   b. Lee Chapman ☐
   c. Tony Gale ☐
   d. Martin Allen ☐

5. When Paul Goddard broke his leg - Which player was pushed up front to play with Tony Cottee scoring 46 league goals between them?
   a. Lee Chapman ☐
   b. Iain Dowie ☐
   c. Frank McAvennie ☐
   d. Trevor Morley ☐

6. Owing a lot to this strike partnership the 85/86 West Ham team recorded their highest ever final league position– which remains to this day. Where did they finish?

    a. 1st ☐

    b. 2nd ☐

    c. 3rd ☐

    d. 5th ☐

7. West Ham were relegated to Division two after the 1988/89 season with just 38 points. Which two North East clubs went down too?

    a. Newcastle and Sunderland ☐

    b. Newcastle and Middlesbrough ☐

    c. Sunderland and Middlesbrough ☐

    d. Sunderland and Hartlepool ☐

8. West Ham changed their manager on 3rd July 1989 when Lou Macari joined the club - his tenure was quite short and ended on 18th February 1990 – what was the reason for this?

    a. West Ham were bottom of the league ☐

    b. He left to join Arsenal ☐

    c. He was being investigated for betting irregularities ☐

    d. The players complained about him ☐

9. Though Macari's tenure was short – he brought in several players who would go on to play an important role for West Ham. Including this striker who scored 57 league goals in 178 games before heading to Norway.

    a. Lee Chapman ☐

    b. Trevor Morley ☐

    c. Ian Rush ☐

    d. Jan Molby ☐

10. Which band released a cover version of "I'm Forever Blowing Bubbles" in 1980?

    a. Black Lace ☐

    b. Iron Maiden ☐

    c. Cockney Rejects ☐

    d. The Clash ☐

(ANSWERS CAN BE FOUND ON PAGE 86)

SCOTTISH HAMMERS

West Ham have had over 30 Scottish players represent the club – can you name the following 10 with help from the clues provided?

1. A towering Centre back – he only played 22 games for West Ham between 2004 and 2005 scoring 2 goals. He went on to play for Watford and his initials are MM.

2. A wand of a left foot. This Scottish International was brought to the club hastily to replace Dimitri Payet in 2017. A difficult task for anyone but he gave his all and scored 11 goals in 86 Hammers appearances before departing to permanently join West Bromwich Albion in 2020

3. With initials BF this goalkeeper played 276 times for West Ham between 1967 and 1980. He was capped by Scotland 7 times and finished his career in Australia with Adelaide City.

4. A full back who scored 84 goals (including 78 penalties) in 434 West Ham games – he won the FA cup with West Ham in 1980 and spent 12 years at the club - he played 10 times for Scotland and spent six years managing in Scotland between 1998 and 2004.

5. A Right back who made his debut for West Ham in 2020 at just 18 years old wearing the squad number 50. Initials HA

6. A striker that had two spells at the club between 1985 and 1992 scored 60 goals in 190 appearances. Suffered a broken leg in his second spell at the club as a result of a challenge from Chris Kamara on the opening day of the 89/90 season

7. Signed for West Ham from West Bromwich Albion in 2007. He was signed by Alan Curbishley to add competition to the central midfield area. He only made eight appearances whilst at the club due to a persistent foot injury and spent some time out on loan. He returned to his boyhood club Queens Park Rangers at the end of his West Ham contract.

8. Curly haired Centre back signed from Blackburn Rovers in 2000. He made 191 appearances for the club before departing in 2007 to join Southampton. He played 67 times for Scotland scoring six goals.

```
┌─────────────────────────────────────┐
│                                     │
│                                     │
└─────────────────────────────────────┘
```

9. Initials TM was a backup goalkeeper to Phil Parkes between 1981 and 1989 playing 85 league games for the club. Never capped by Scotland he had a spell on loan at Colchester United at the end of his spell with West Ham.

```
┌─────────────────────────────────────┐
│                                     │
│                                     │
└─────────────────────────────────────┘
```

10. He had two spells at West Ham the first between 1994 and 1996 then returned in 2001 when he stayed at the club until 2005 before departing to join Millwall. A committed central midfielder who scored 11 goals in 27 appearances in his first spell at the club. He played 26 times for Scotland scoring 6 goals

```
┌─────────────────────────────────────┐
│                                     │
│                                     │
└─────────────────────────────────────┘
```

SECTION TWELVE

WEST HAM UNITED 1990s

1. Which tough tackling left back was club Captain at the start of the 90/91 season?
   - a. Steve Potts ☐
   - b. Scott Minto ☐
   - c. Ray Stewart ☐
   - d. Julian Dicks ☐
2. Lou Macari departed the club on 18th February 1990. Which West Ham Legend became manager for the next four years?
   - a. Geoff Hurst ☐
   - b. Billy Bonds ☐
   - c. Frank Lampard Sr ☐
   - d. Bobby Moore ☐

3. Under new management West Ham gained promotion to the top division finishing 2nd in the 90/91 season. They also had a run in the FA cup eventually losing in the semi-final to Nottingham Forest. With the scores at 0-0 which player was sent off after just 20 minutes?

   a. Tony Gale ☐

   b. Julian Dicks ☐

   c. Trevor Morley ☐

   d. Martin Allen ☐

4. What controversial scheme was introduced in 1991 as West Ham looked to redevelop the ground considering the Lord Justice Taylor report following the Hillsborough disaster?

   a. The Supporters Trust Scheme ☐

   b. Season Ticket Scheme ☐

   c. The box office scheme ☐

   d. The Bond Scheme ☐

5. West Ham were relegated at the end of the 91/92 season meaning they missed out on the first season of the newly formed Premier League that started in 1992. What was the outcome of West Hams 92/93 season?

    a. Champions ☐

    b. Automatic Promotion finishing 2nd ☐

    c. Promotion via Play offs ☐

    d. Play off Final defeat ☐

6. In 1994 which former hammer became manager of the club?

    a. Martin Peters ☐

    b. John Sissons ☐

    c. Harry Redknapp ☐

    d. Bryan Robson ☐

7. On 31st January 1996 at 17 years of age which youth product made the first of 187 appearances for the club when he came on to replace John Moncur – he scored 37 goals for West Ham

    a. Frank Lampard jr ☐

    b. Joe Cole ☐

    c. Michael Carrick ☐

    d. Rio Ferdinand ☐

8. Who was named as club captain in 1997 and remained until 2001? A hardworking midfielder signed from Manchester City for £2.5 million who played 227 games for the club.

    a. John Moncur ☐

    b. Steve Lomas ☐

    c. Trevor Sinclair ☐

    d. Marc Vivien-Foe ☐

9. In January 1999 West Ham signed what Italian from Sheffield Wednesday? An instant fan favourite and remains a legend at the football club.

    a. Benito Carbone ☐

    b. Simone Zaza ☐

    c. Paolo Di Canio ☐

    d. David Di Michele ☐

10. What European competition did West Ham win in 1999 defeating Metz and winning 3-2 on aggregate

    a. Cup Winners Cup ☐

    b. European Cup ☐

    c. Inter-toto Cup ☐

    d. Europa League ☐

(ANSWERS CAN BE FOUND ON PAGE 88)

SECTION THIRTEEN

WEST HAM UNITED 1999
CUP FINAL XI

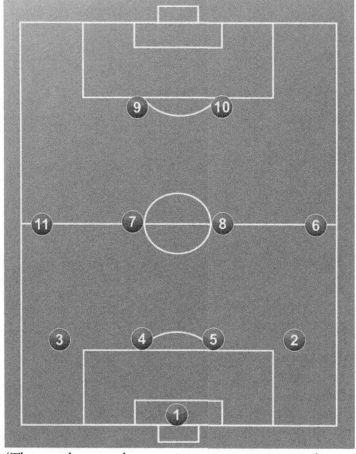

(The numbers used are to represent positions only – they are not accurate as worn on the day)

How many of the West Ham 1999 CUP XI final winners can you name? This refers to the second leg that was won 3-1

1. SH	
2. SP	
3. MK	
4. RF	
5. SL	
6. MVF	
7. JM	
8. FL	
9. PDC	
10. PW	
11. TS	

Bonus points. Can you name the substitute used?

12. JC	

(ANSWERS CAN BE FOUND ON PAGE 89)

WEST HAM UNITED 2000s

1. Who was appointed manager of West Ham in 2001?
    a. Ray Clemence ☐
    b. Lee Chapman ☐
    c. Glenn Roeder ☐
    d. George Burley ☐

2. Who signed for a club record fee of £5.5 million in September 2001?
    a. Vladimir Labant ☐
    b. Lee Bowyer ☐
    c. Tomas Repka ☐
    d. Marlon Harewood ☐

3. In the 2002/03 season West Ham were relegated with a record high point total. How many points did they accrue?

    a. 39 ☐

    b. 40 ☐

    c. 42 ☐

    d. 44 ☐

4. West Ham changed manager again in 2003. An ex-Crystal Palace player who had been in charge of Reading FC was appointed. What was his name?

    a. Alan Pardew ☐

    b. Steve Bruce ☐

    c. Roy Hodgson ☐

    d. Tony Pulis ☐

5. West Ham secured promotion via the play offs in 2005. Who scored the winning goal against Preston North End at the Millennium stadium in Cardiff?

    a. Mark Noble ☐

    b. Hayden Mullins ☐

    c. Bobby Zamora ☐

    d. Matthew Etherington ☐

6. In 2005 a legendary Premier League striker joined the club who had won the league three times. Who was he?

   a. Andy Cole ☐

   b. Chris Sutton ☐

   c. Alan Shearer ☐

   d. Teddy Sheringham ☐

7. West Ham spent £7 million on a striker from Norwich in January 2006. He scored 19 goals in 56 games for West Ham. He suffered a broken ankle whilst on England duty in August 2006 and missed the 2006/7 season

   a. Malky Mackay ☐

   b. Brian Deane ☐

   c. Darren Huckerby ☐

   d. Dean Ashton ☐

8. In 2006 West Ham signed a striker from Chelsea. A hardworking player who although not prolific was West Hams top goalscorer in the Premier league in 08/09 and 09/10

   a. Frederic Kanoute ☐

   b. Marlon Harewood ☐

   c. Carlton Cole ☐

   d. Sergiy Rebrov☐

9. Who did West Ham lose to in the 2006 FA cup Final?

    a. Southampton ☐

    b. Liverpool ☐

    c. Manchester City ☐

    d. Arsenal ☐

10. Which Argentinian joined West Ham alongside Carlos Tevez in 2006 in a move that come under much scrutiny?

    a. Mauricio Tarrico ☐

    b. Javier Margas ☐

    c. Gabriel Batistuta ☐

    d. Javier Mascherano☐

(ANSWERS CAN BE FOUND ON PAGE 90)

SECTION FIFTEEN

WEST HAM UNITED 2006 FA CUP FINAL XI

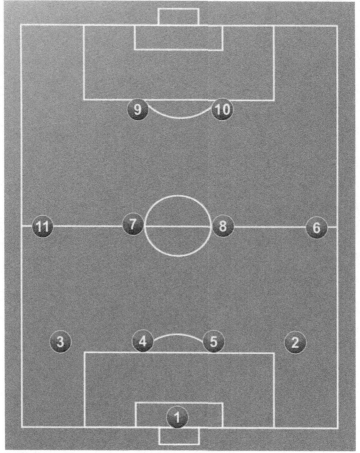

(The numbers used are to represent positions only – they are not accurate as worn on the day)

Can you name the 2006 FA CUP FINAL XI?

1. SH	
2. LS	
3. PK	
4. DG	
5. AF	
6. CF	
7. YB	
8. NRC	
9. DA	
10. MH	
11. ME	

Can you also name the three substitutes used

12. BZ	
13. CD	
14. TS	

(ANSWERS CAN BE FOUND ON PAGE 91)

SECTION SIXTEEN

WEST HAM UNITED 2010s

1. In January 2010 which duo took a 50% stake in the club?
    a. Hendry and O'sullivan ☐
    b. Brady and Peschisolido ☐
    c. Gold and Sullivan ☐
    d. Hale and Pace ☐
2. Who took over from Avram Grant as manager in June 2011 and spent three seasons as manager?
    a. Gianfranco Zola ☐
    b. Alan Curbishley ☐
    c. Slaven Bilic ☐
    d. Sam Allardyce ☐

3. In May 2012 West Ham headed to Wembley to compete in the play-off final against Blackpool. The hammers came out as 2-1 winners thanks to an 87th minute goal from which player?

   a. Ricardo Vaz Te ☐

   b. Carlton Cole ☐

   c. Kevin Nolan ☐

   d. Jack Collison ☐

4. Who was signed from Liverpool in August 2012 initially on-loan before completing a permanent transfer the following season?

   a. Matt Jarvis ☐

   b. Andy Carroll ☐

   c. Yossi Benayoun ☐

   d. John Carew ☐

5. 2015 which loyal hammer was name as club captain? He had made his debut in 2004 at the age of 17

   a. Mark Noble ☐

   b. Aaron Cresswell ☐

   c. James Tomkins ☐

   d. Reece Oxford ☐

6. Which Romanian team knocked West Ham out of the Europa League Play off and qualifying rounds in 2015 and 2016
   a. Rapid Bucuresti ☐
   b. Astra Giurgiu ☐
   c. CFR Cluj ☐
   d. FC Steaua Bucuresti ☐

7. Slaven Bilic was appointed West Ham manager in June 2015. Where had he been managing prior to joining West Ham?
   a. Hajduk Split ☐
   b. Besiktas ☐
   c. Everton ☐
   d. Lokomotiv Moscow ☐

8. Name the French playmaker who signed for the club in June 2015. Despite a relatively short spell at the club his exceptional footballing ability will be remembered for a long time
   a. Modibo Maiga ☐
   b. Florian Thauvin ☐
   c. Victor Moses ☐
   d. Dimitri Payet ☐

9. West Ham played their last match at Upton Park on 10th May 2016 against Manchester United. West Ham fought back to win 3-2. Who scored the winning goal?

    a. Andy Carroll ☐

    b. Michail Antonio ☐

    c. Winston Reid ☐

    d. Diafra Sakho ☐

10. The first competitive fixture at the London Stadium on 4th August 2016 was in the Europa league against NK Domzale in front of 53,914. Who scored the opening goal that day?

    a. Mark Noble ☐

    b. Sofiane Feghouli ☐

    c. Andy Carroll ☐

    d. Cheikou Kouyate ☐

(ANSWERS CAN BE FOUND ON PAGE 92)

WEST HAM UNITED
2012 CHAMPIONSHIP PLAY OFF
FINAL XI

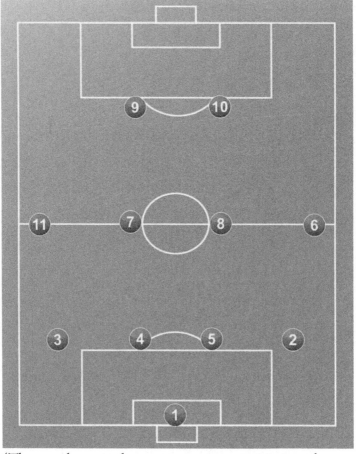

(The numbers used are to represent positions only – they are not accurate as worn on the day)

West Ham 2012 CHAMPIONSHIP PLAY OFF FINAL XI can you name them? Initials provided

1. RG	
2. GD	
3. MT	
4. WR	
5. JT	
6. MN	
7. JC	
8. KN	
9. CC	
10. GO'N	
11. RVT	

Can you also name the two substitutes?

12. GM	
13. JF	

(ANSWERS CAN BE FOUND ON PAGE 93)

WEST HAM UNITED 2020s

1. In July 2020 Eintracht Frankfurt reported West Ham to FIFA for failing to pay instalments on which player that was purchased for £45 million in 2019?
    a. Felipe Anderson ☐
    b. Sebastian Haller ☐
    c. Nikola Vlasic ☐
    d. Pablo Fornals ☐

2. In July 2020 which Czech Player joined West Ham for £15 million from Slavia Prague?
    a. Tomas Soucek ☐
    b. Vladimir Coufal ☐
    c. Albian Ajeti ☐
    d. Said Benrahma ☐

3. Which promising young player left the club in 2020 to join West Bromwich Albion much to the disappointment of the fans and some players?

    a. Conor Coventry ☐

    b. Jordan Hugill ☐

    c. Josh Cullen ☐

    d. Grady Diangana ☐

4. What youth product made his 100th Premier League appearance on 29th February 2020?

    a. Mark Noble ☐

    b. Declan Rice ☐

    c. Ben Johnson ☐

    d. Aaron Cresswell ☐

5. What player signed for West Ham on loan on 29th January 2021 scoring 9 goals in just 16 Premier League games

    a. Jesse Lingard ☐

    b. Said Benrahma ☐

    c. Jarrod Bowen ☐

    d. Andriy Yarmolenko ☐

6. In the 2020/21 season what position did West Ham finish in the table to qualify for the Europa league?

    a. 4th ☐

    b. 5th ☐

    c. 6th ☐

    d. 7th ☐

7. The 2021/22 season saw West Hams first appearance in the Europa League group stage. Who were the first opponents they played on the 15th September 2021?

    a. Lazio ☐

    b. Anderlecht ☐

    c. Sparta Prague ☐

    d. Dinamo Zagreb ☐

8. On the 14th April 2022 West Ham produced their best display in Europa for decades with an impressive 3-0 win away to which French team?

    a. Monaco ☐

    b. Montpellier ☐

    c. Lyon ☐

    d. Marseille ☐

9. Despite defeat in the semi-final of the Europa
    League against Eintracht Frankfurt two West
    Ham players were named in the Europa
    League Team of the Season Declan Rice and
    ....?

    a. Michail Antonio ☐

    b. Aaron Cresswell ☐

    c. Jarrod Bowen ☐

    d. Craig Dawson ☐

10. Who finished as West Hams top goalscorer in
    the 21/22 season with 18 goals in all
    competitions?

    a. Michail Antonio ☐

    b. Said Benrahma ☐

    c. Jarrod Bowen ☐

    d. Tomas Soucek ☐

(ANSWERS CAN BE FOUND ON PAGE 94)

WEST HAM UNITED
07.06.23 CONFERENCE LEAGUE
FINAL STARTING XI

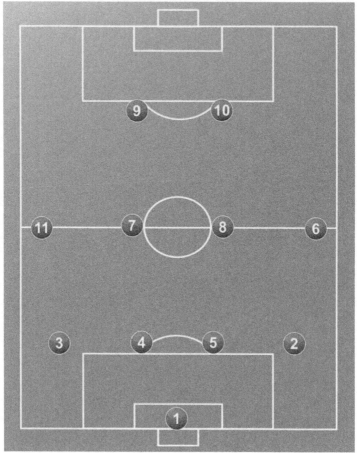

(The numbers used are to represent positions only – they are not accurate as worn on the day)

How many of the West Ham 2023 CONFERENCE LEAGUE FINAL TEAM can you name? Initials provided to assist

1. AA	
2. VC	
3. EP	
4. KZ	
5. NA	
6. DR	
7. TS	
8. LP	
9. MA	
10.JB	
11.SB	

(ANSWERS CAN BE FOUND ON PAGE 95)

Crossword 13 clues. Players surnames only

2. Manager who won the FA cup in 1980

7. regarded as west hams best ever player

8. Top Premier League Goalscorer

9. Legenary Czech Goalkeeper

10. Signed from Hull City in 2020

11. Italian signed from Sheffield Wednesday

13. West Hams oldest ever player

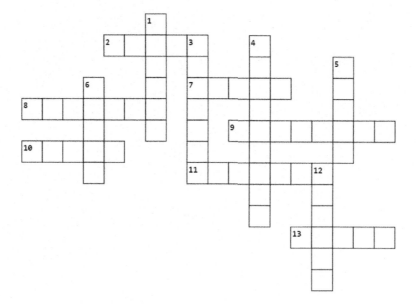

1. Who is West Hams top all time goalscorer?

3. Father and son both played for the club

4. Who was sold to Leeds in 2001?

5. England 1966 hattrick hero

6. Managed the club in to spells 2017 and 2019

12. West Hams youngest ever Debutant?

(ANSWERS CAN BE FOUND ON PAGE 96)

ANSWERS

Section one: Early History of West Ham United

1. C – 1895

2. B – The Memorial Grounds

3. B – 1904

4. C – The Castle

5. C – Millwall

6. C – Syd King

7. B – Southern Football League

8. C – 1923

9. B – Vic Watson

10. A – Jimmy Ruffell

/10

ANSWERS

Section TWO name the famous Hammer

1. Julian Dicks

2. David Cross

3. Ludek Miklosko

4. Kevin Nolan

5. Matt Jarvis

6. Rio Ferdinand

7. Billy Bonds

8. Scott Parker

9. Michail Antonio

10. John Moncur

/10

ANSWERS

Section Three: West Ham 1980 FA CUP FINAL XI

1. PP   Phil Parkes

2. RS   Ray Stewart

3. FL   Frank Lampard

4. BB   Billy Bonds

5. AM   Alvin Martin

6. AD   Alan Devonshire

7. PA   Paul Allen

8. SP   Stuart Pearson

9. DC   David Cross

10. TB   Trevor Brooking

11. GP   Geoff Pike

12. PB   Paul Brush

/12

ANSWERS

Section four: West Ham United 1920s-1950s

1. D – 1923

2. C – Bolton Wanderers 2-0 West Ham United

3. B – Clapton Orient

4. C – The White Horse Final

5. D – 20th

6. D – Football League War Cup

7. C – It was partially destroyed by a German Bomb

8. C – Ted Fenton

9. D – Discussing match tactics and formations

10. B – Bobby Moore

/10

ANSWERS

SECTION FIVE

Section FIVE: Five clues to name the hammers player

Remember points awarded depending on what clue you got the correct answer on:

1. Stan Lazaridis

2. Ricardo Vaz Te

3. Dimitri Payet

4. Neil Ruddock

5. Joe Cole

FIVE points awarded if you got the correct answer after the first clue. FOUR points awarded if you got the correct answer after the second clue. THREE points awarded if you got the correct answer after the third clue. TWO points awarded if you got the correct answer after the fourth clue. ONE point awarded if you needed all five clues to get the correct answer

/25

ANSWERS

Section SIX – West Ham United 1960s

1. A – Ron Greenwood

2. C – Preston North End

3. D – Ronnie Boyce

4. B – Winners

5. A – Sports Personality Team of the year award

6. D – Jimmy Greaves

7. A – 41

8. B – The Chicken Run

9. D – 100

10. A – Tottenham Hotspur

/10

ANSWERS

Section SEVEN – West Ham Player Nicknames

1. D - Julian Dicks

2. B – Bryan Robson

3. C – Neil Ruddock

4. A – James Collins

5. D – Ray Stewart

6. B – Thomas Hitzlsperger

7. D – Fabian Balbuena

8. A – Javier Hernandez

9. D – David Unsworth

10. A – Fitz Hall

/10

ANSWERS

Section EIGHT – West Ham United 1970s

1. A – Bryan Robson

2. B – John Lyall

3. C – Fulham

4. C – Billy Bonds

5. D – Alan Taylor

6. C – Anderlecht

7. D – Francois Van Der Elst

8. A – Alan Devonshire

9. C – West Ham were relegated

10. D – Phil Parkes

/10

ANSWERS

Section NINE – West Ham England Internationals

1. Trevor Brooking

2. Alvin Martin

3. Rio Ferdinand

4. Joe Cole

5. David James

6. Trevor Sinclair

7. Matthew Upson

8. Rob Green

9. Declan Rice

10. Alan Devonshire

/10

ANSWERS

Section TEN – West Ham 1980s

1. C – First time a club outside the top tier won the FA CUP

2. D – 10-0

3. D – Alvin Martin

4. C – Tony Gale

5. C – Frank McAvennie

6. C – 3rd

7. B – Newcastle and Middlesbrough

8. C – He was being investigated for betting irregularities

9. B – Trevor Morley

10. C – Cockney Rejects

/10

ANSWERS

Section ELEVEN – Scottish Hammers

1. Malky Mackay

2. Robert Snodgrass

3. Bobby Ferguson

4. Ray Stewart

5. Harrison Ashby

6. Frank McAvennie

7. Nigel Quashie

8. Christian Dailly

9. Tom McAllister

10. Don Hutchison

/10

Section TWELVE – West Ham United 1990s

1. D – Julian Dicks

2. B – Billy Bonds

3. A – Tony Gale

4. D – The Bond Scheme

5. B – Automatic Promotion finishing 2nd

6. C – Harry Redknapp

7. A – Frank Lampard

8. B – Steve Lomas

9. C – Paolo Di Canio

10. C – Inter-toto Cup

/10

ANSWERS

SECTION THIRTEEN

WEST HAM UNITED 1999 UEFA XI

1. SH	Shaka Hislop
2. SP	Steve Potts
3. MK	Marc Keller
4. RF	Rio Ferdinand
5. SL	Steve Lomas
6. MVF	Marc Vivien Foe
7. JM	John Moncur
8. FL	Frank Lampard
9. PDC	Paolo Di Canio
10. PW	Paulo Wanchope
11. TS	Trevor Sinclair
12. JC	Joe Cole

/12

SECTION FOURTEEN - WEST HAM UNITED 2000s

1. C – Glenn Roeder

2. C – Tomas Repka

3. C – 42 points

4. A – Alan Pardew

5. C – Bobby Zamora

6. D – Teddy Sheringham

7. D – Dean Ashton

8. C – Carlton Cole

9. B – Liverpool

10. D – Javier Mascherano

/10

Section FIFTEEN – West Ham United 2006 FA CUP FINAL XI

1.	SH	Shaka Hislop
2.	LS	Lionel Scaloni
3.	PK	Paul Konchesky
4.	DG	Danny Gabbidon
5.	AF	Anton Ferdinand
6.	CF	Carl Fletcher
7.	YB	Yossi Benayoun
8.	NRC	Nigel Reo-Coker
9.	DA	Dean Ashton
10.	MH	Marlon Harewood
11.	ME	Matthew Etherington
12.	BZ	Bobby Zamora
13.	CD	Christian Dailly
14.	TS	Teddy Sheringham

/14

SECTION SIXTEEN - WEST HAM UNITED 2010s

1. C – Gold and Sullivan

2. D – Sam Allardyce

3. A – Ricard Vaz Te

4. B – Andy Carroll

5. A – Mark Noble

6. B – Astra Giurgiu

7. B – Besiktas

8. D – Dimitri Payet

9. C – Winston Reid

10. D – Cheikou Kouyate

/10

ANSWERS

SECTION SEVENTEEN

WEST HAM UNITED 2012 PLAY OFF FINAL XI

1. Rob Green
2. Guy Demel
3. Matt Taylor
4. Winston Reid
5. James Tomkins
6. Mark Noble
7. Jack Collison
8. Kevin Nolan
9. Carlton Cole
10. Gary ONeil
11. Ricardo Vaz Te
12. George McCartney
13. Julian Faubert

/13

SECTION EIGHTEEN
WEST HAM UNITED
2020-2023

1. B – Sebastian Haller

2. A – Tomas Soucek

3. D – Grady Diangana

4. B – Declan Rice

5. A - Jesse Lingard

6. C – 6th

7. D – Dinamo Zagreb

8. C – Lyon

9. D – Craig Dawson

10. C – Jarrod Bowen

/10

ANSWERS

SECTION NINETEEN

WEST HAM UNITED
CONFERENCE LEAGUE FINAL XI

1. Alphonse Areola
2. Vladimir Coufal
3. Emerson Palmieri
4. Kurt Zouma
5. Nayef Aguerd
6. Declan Rice
7. Tomas Soucek
8. Lucas Paqueta
9. Michail Antonio
10. Jarrod Bowen
11. Said Benrahma

/11

SECTION TWENTY

SURNAMES ONLY CROSSWORD ANSWERS

ACROSS

2. LYALL

7. MOORE

8. ANTONIO

9. MIKLOSKO

10. BOWEN

11. DICANIO

13. BONDS

DOWN

1. WATSON

3. LAMPARD

4. FERDINAND

5. HURST

6. MOYES

12. OXFORD

/13

That completes the quiz and with a total of 230 points available – where do you stand?

210-230 MASSIVE HAMMER

201-209 Boleyn Born and Bred

151-200 East Ender and Proud

100-150 Academy of football but must improve

51-99 Still learning the ropes

0-50 Are you Millwall in disguise???

Hopefully you have enjoyed this little quiz book and it has been a challenge but your knowledge has extended and been rewarded. Now it's time to challenge your friends and family. Challenge the ardent fan that claims they know everything and see whether they are a MASSIVE HAMMER or a closet Millwall fan.

Take away multiple choice options for the easier questions and use the book to teach the next generation of fans about the history of our great club.

Printed in Great Britain
by Amazon

33105086R00057